My Hypermobility

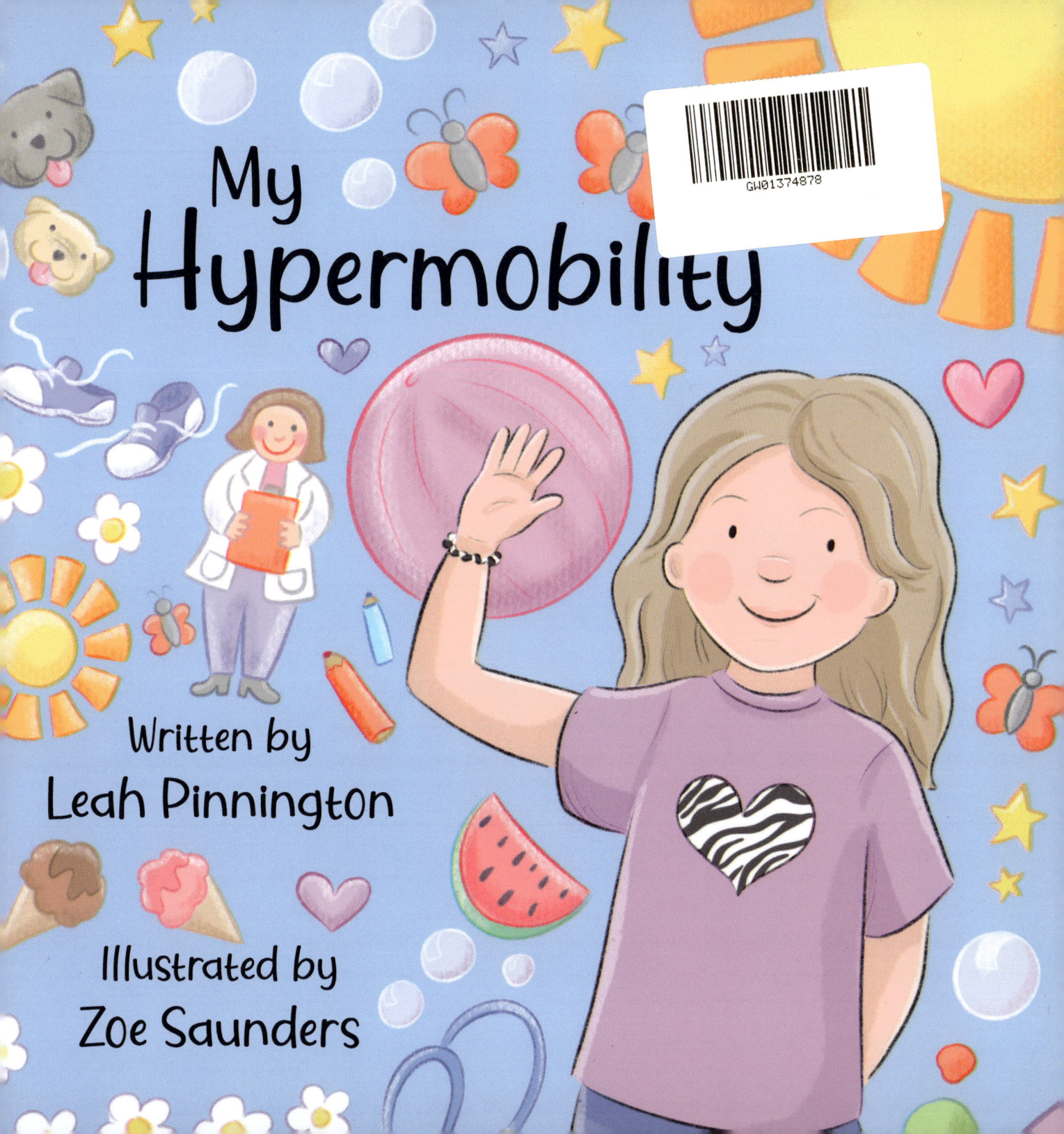

Written by
Leah Pinnington

Illustrated by
Zoe Saunders

Copyright © 2024 Leah Pinnington. All rights reserved.
Cover and illustrations by Zoe Saunders.

No part of this publication may be reproduced in whole or in part, or stored in a retrieval system, or transmitted by any means, electronic, mechanical, photocopying, recording or otherwise, without written permission of the author.

A CIP catalogue record for this book is available from the British Library.

Published in 2024 by Pinnington Publishing.

Paperback ISBN: 978-1-7384372-0-7
Hardcover ISBN: 978-1-7384372-1-4

To my dearest daughter, Rosa.
This book is for you. You have inspired me every step of the way.
Your patience and maturity throughout this journey have been
remarkable. Thank you for lending me your imagination and for
being my constant source of inspiration.

To my treasured daughter, Maia,
Thank you for not only being my beautiful child
but also for being my friend.

To my beloved husband, Craig,
Your support and encouragement have been invaluable to me.
Thank you for standing by my side through this process.

And last but certainly not least, to my loyal companion, Persie,
You may be a furry member of the family but thank you for snuggling
by my side during my writing and creative evenings.

I am grateful for each and every one of you, my amazing family.

With all my love,
Leah.

Hi, I'm Rosa!

I'm guessing you've picked up this book because you're curious about what hypermobility is, or maybe you have hypermobility. If you do, don't worry, you're not alone!

Either way, you've come to the right place.

Grab yourself a cup of water and a fruity snack while I tell you about the last four years of my life.

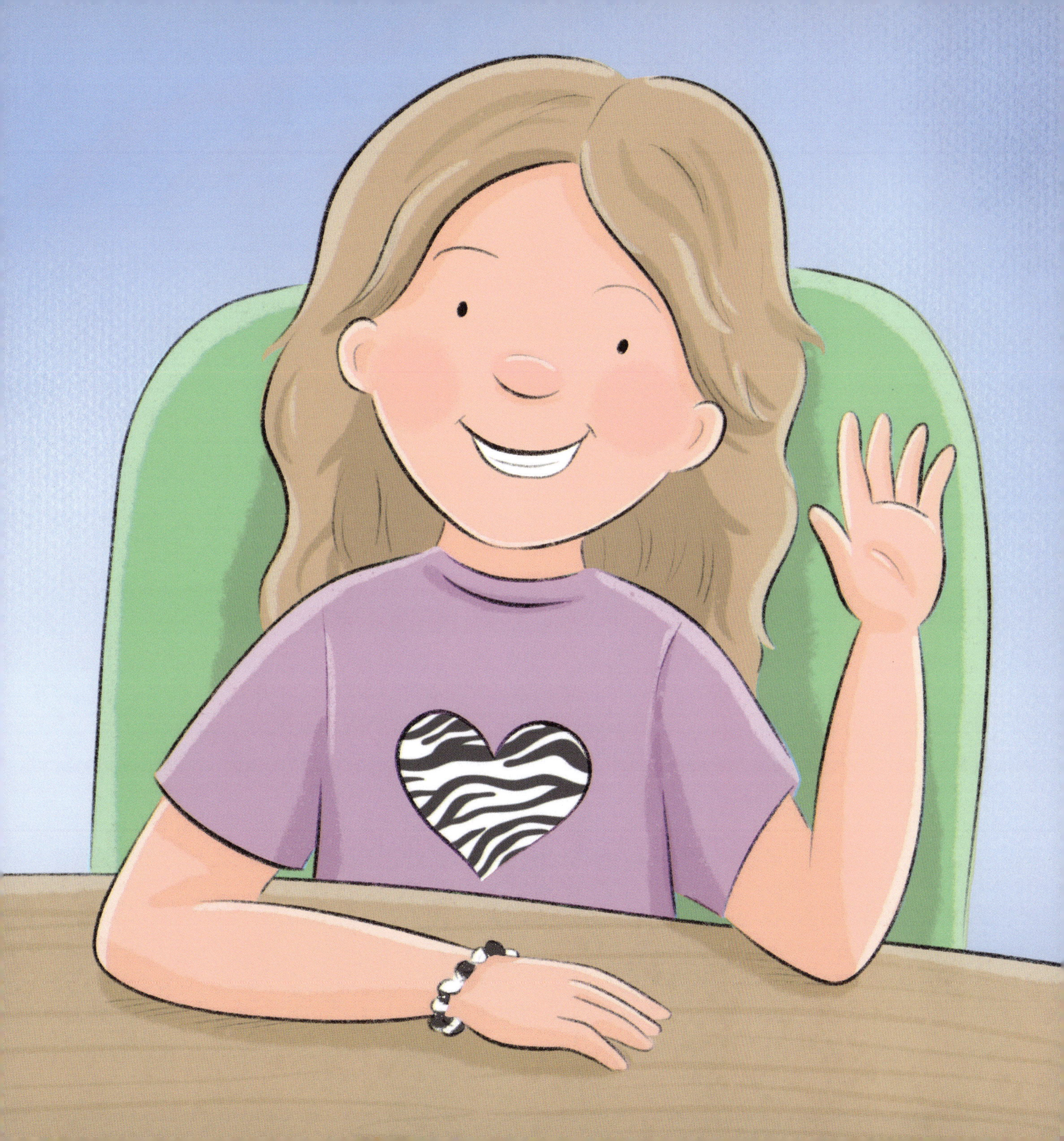

From the outside, my body did not look sore. But on the inside, it was the opposite. My ankles and legs hurt, especially when I walked for too long or competed in lots of physical activities.

I often felt really tired, even after a long sleep. Some days, getting out of bed was difficult because my legs were stiff.

I did not have very good balance or coordination.

I struggled to do small tasks like holding a pen or fastening buttons on my school shirt.

Do you have something similar?

When I was six, I told Mum about my pain, and she took me to the doctor.

Doctors can sometimes feel scary, but they listened to me, which made me feel happy.

The doctor decided that I should have an MRI scan.

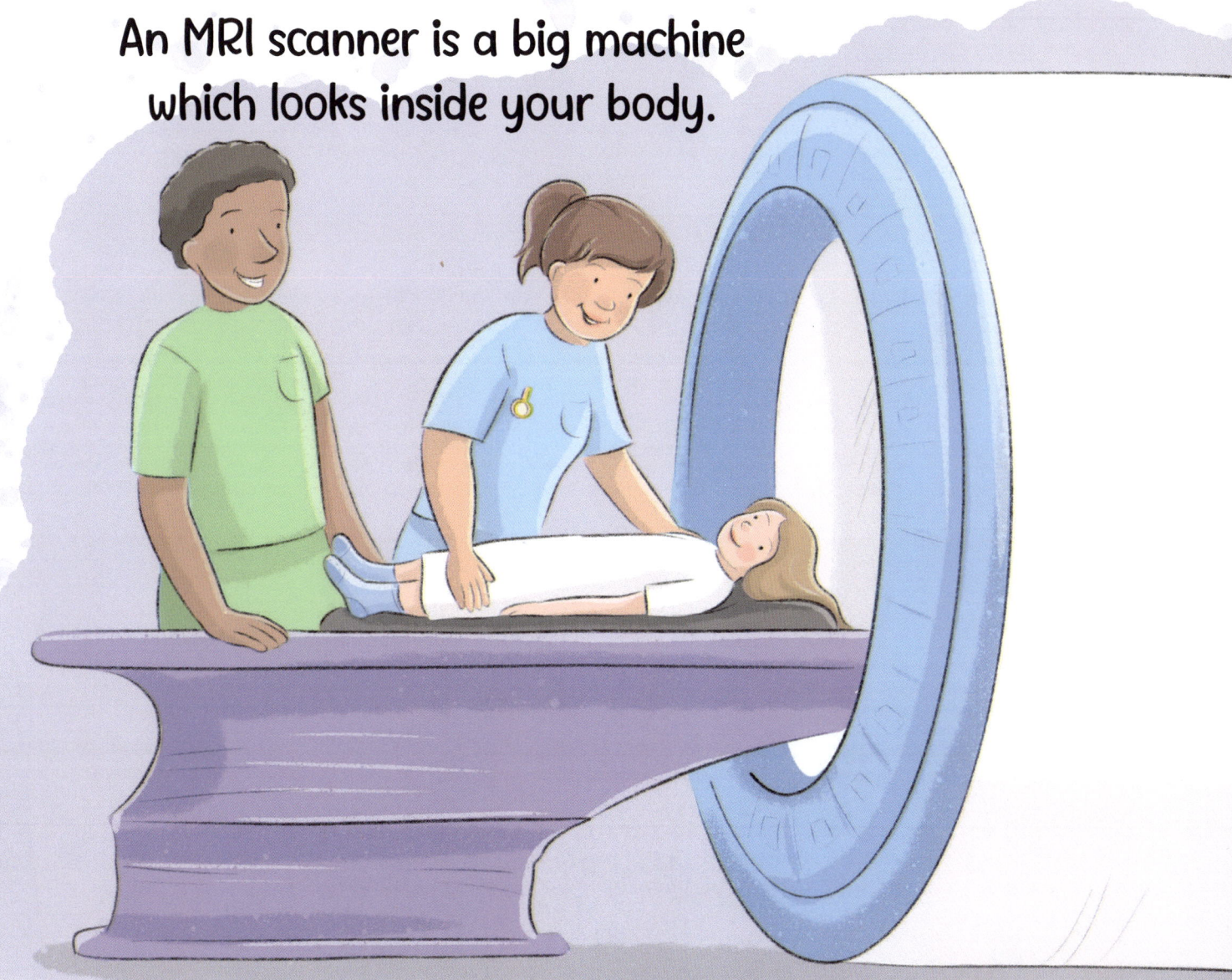

An MRI scanner is a big machine which looks inside your body.

I felt a little nervous, but the nurses and doctors were friendly and made it fun for me.

After further checks at the hospital,
the doctors told me I had joint hypermobility.

This means that I have extra flexible joints, which cause me to feel the way I do.

SYMPTOMS

- OFTEN VERY TIRED (EVEN AFTER A REST)
- WEAKNESS
- ACHES AND PAINS
- TUMMY AND BLADDER PROBLEMS
- LOOSE JOINTS
- JOINT SWELLING
- STRUGGLES TO CONCENTRATE
- STRETCHY SKIN
- JOINT PAIN
- FINE MOTOR DIFFICULTIES
- POOR CO-ORDINATION
- MAY SEEM CLUMSY
- FLAT FEET (FEET TURN IN)

Since my diagnosis, I have attended physiotherapy and occupational therapy at a children's hospital.

My physiotherapist, called Sue, gives me exercises.

Some are fun, and some can be a little boring, but they all make my muscles stronger.

Sometimes, I do my exercises at home.

I use my big yoga ball and play special games with my older sister.

The occupational therapist helps me to develop my finger muscles.

To do this, we use tough slime and practice pressing it into different shapes.

Do you like slime?

Writing can be a bit difficult for me. Because of this, I'm allowed to use my very own laptop at school for longer pieces of written work.

This is super helpful because my fingers ache when I hold my pencil for too long.

Do you get sore fingers too?

To help with the pain and discomfort that I feel in my ankles and legs, I have special insoles in my shoes.

When they were first made at the hospital, they made my feet feel warm and toasty!

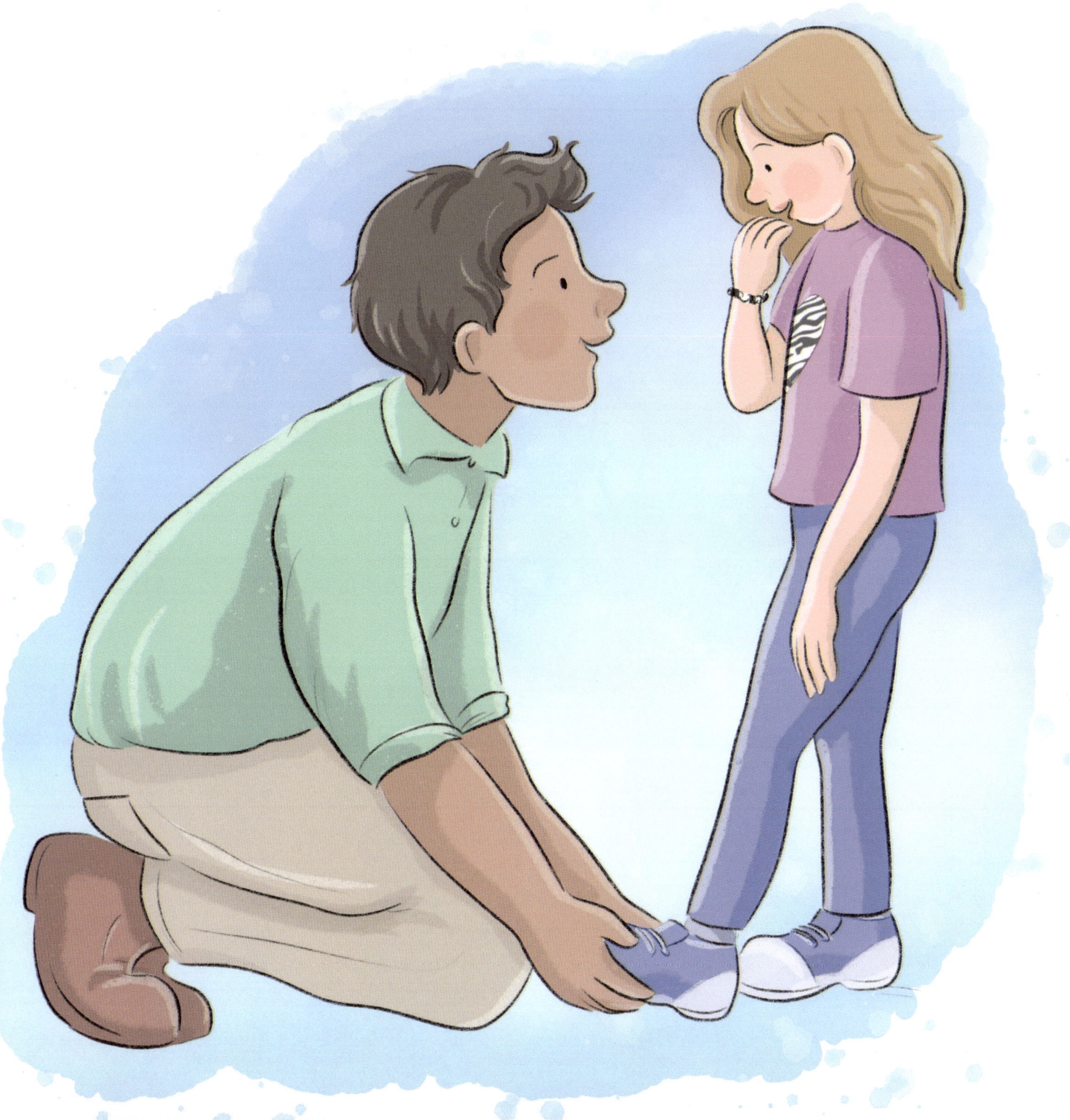

I use lots of day-to-day tricks to help me cope with my hypermobility. One is called "pacing" which lets me rest in school when I need to.

Sometimes, Mum allows me to stop for ice cream breaks when we are out walking, which is a real bonus.

I bet you like ice cream, too.

What's your favourite flavour?

Having a warm bath makes my aches and pains feel better. I like to overload it with bath bombs and bubbles, especially those that turn the water a different colour!

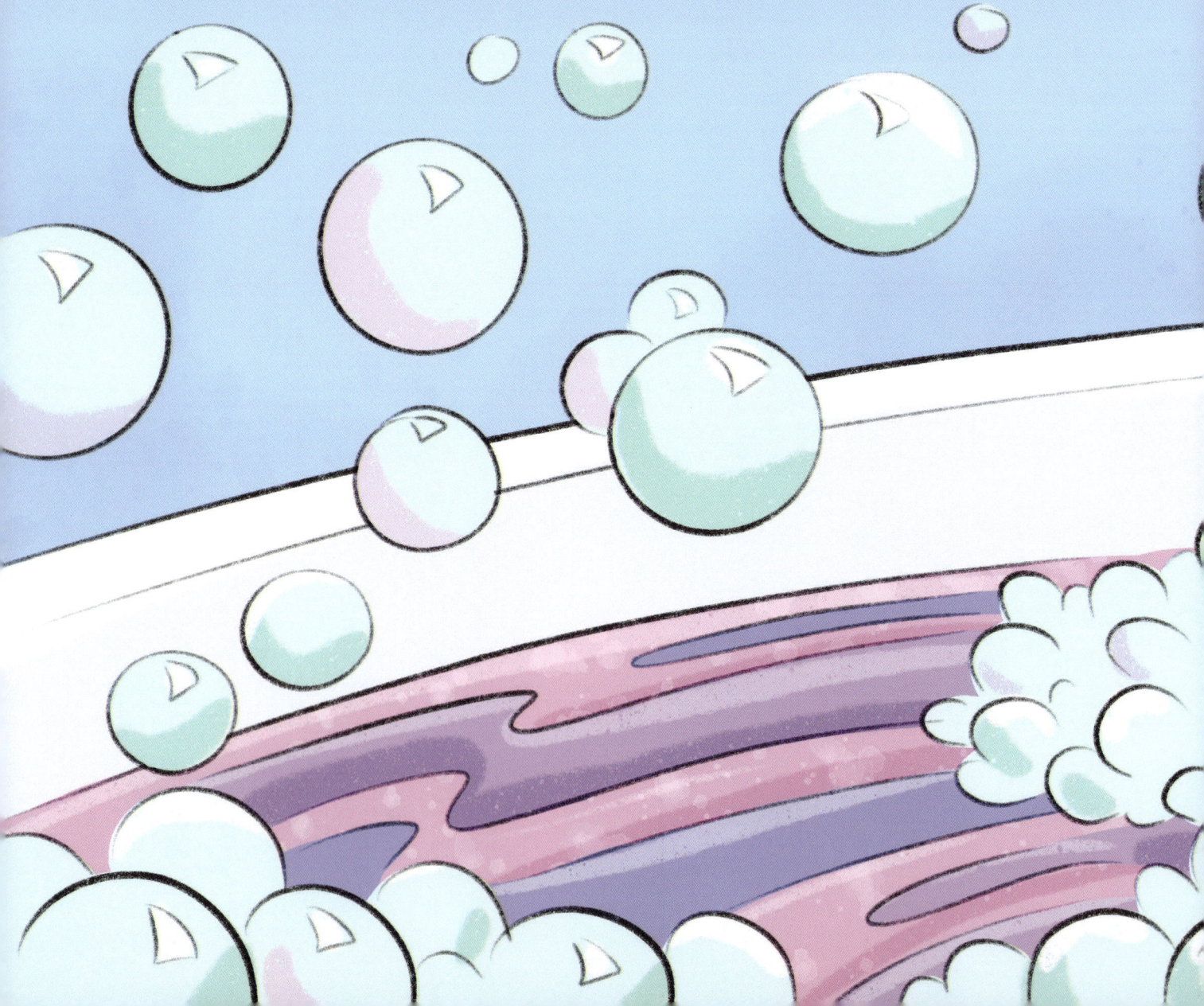

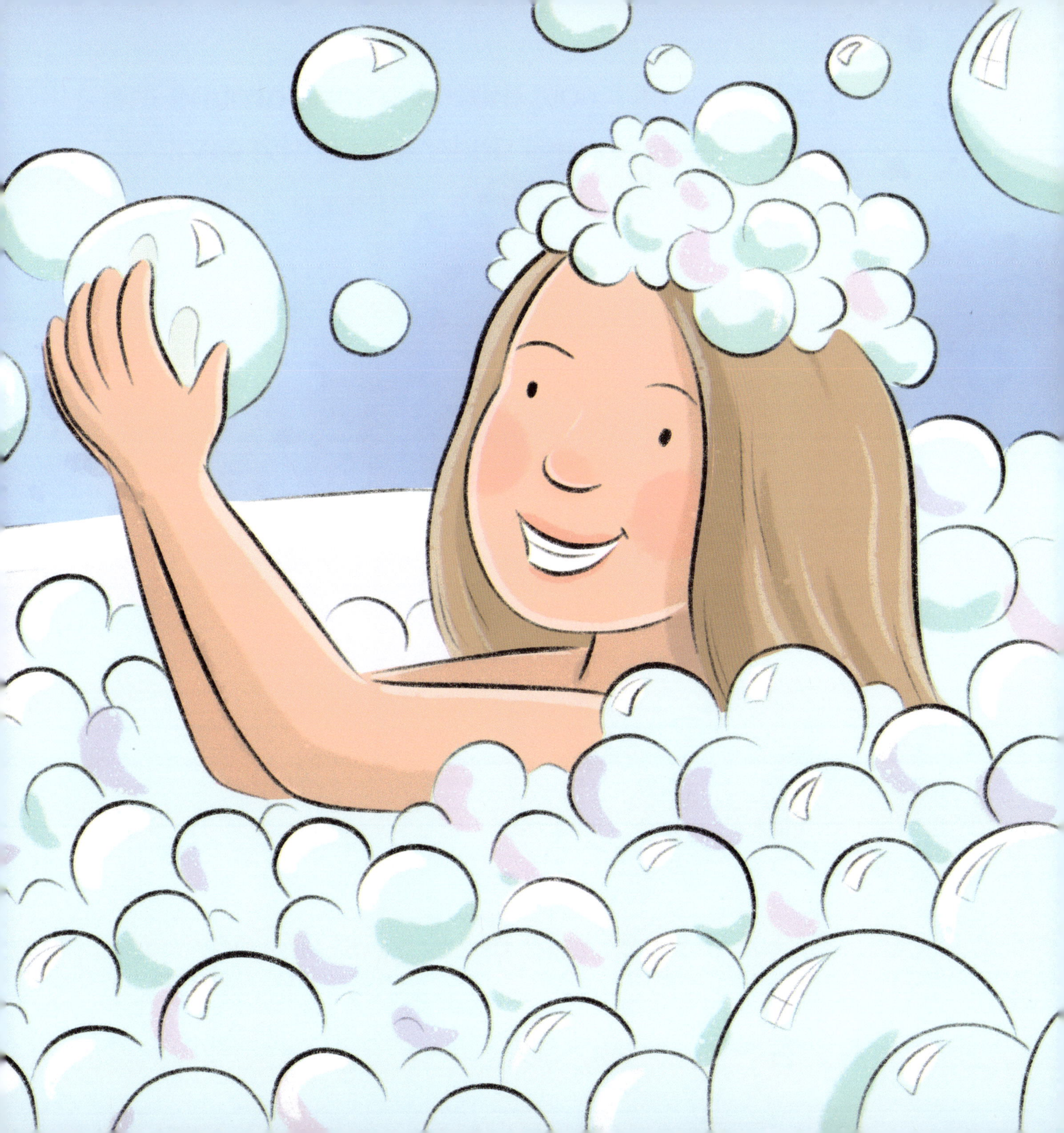

I feel a lot happier now that everyone around me knows how I feel and understands the small struggles I face every day.

I have learnt that talking to your family, friends, and teachers is best. Everyone loves you and wants to help make you feel better.

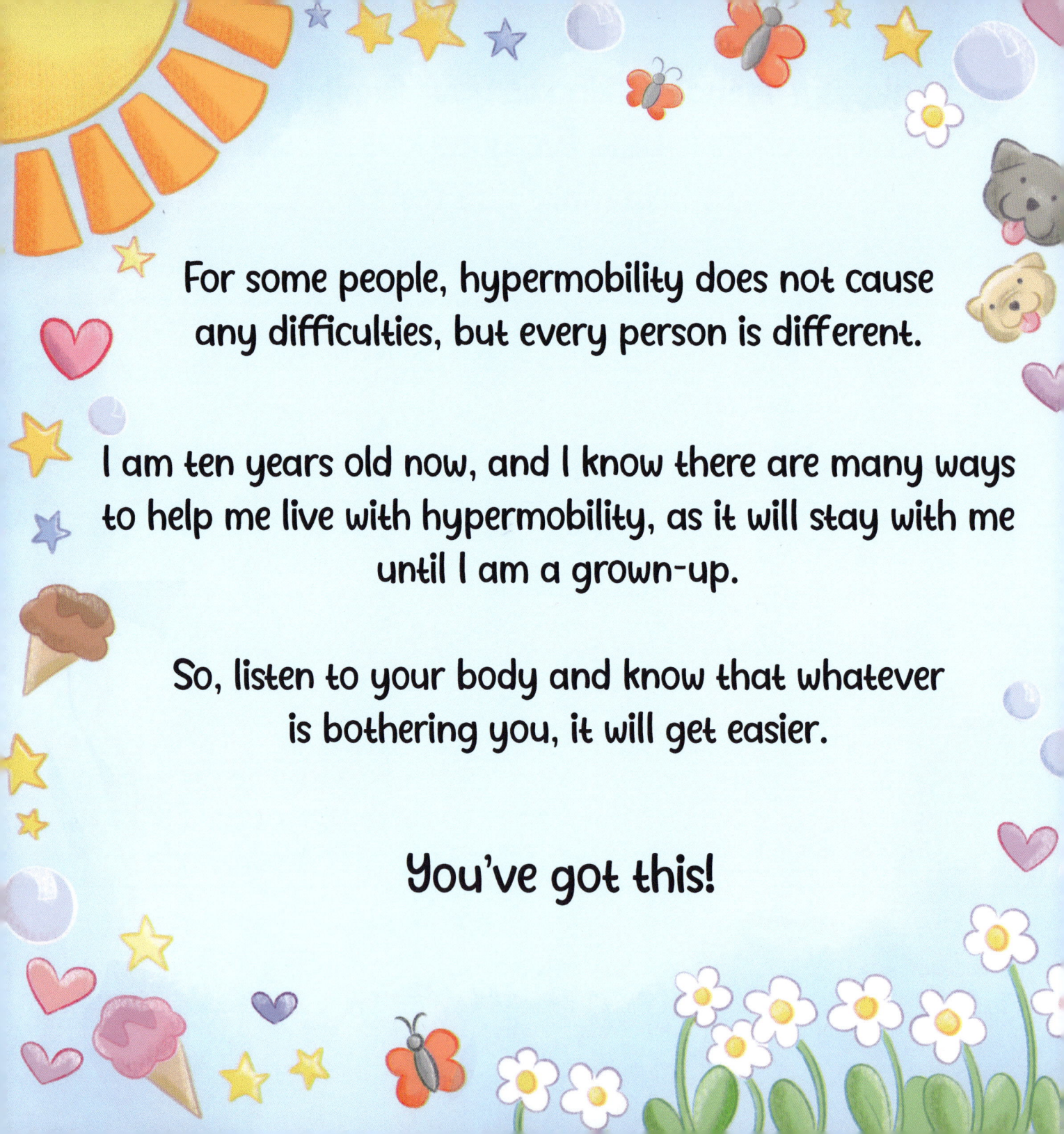

For some people, hypermobility does not cause any difficulties, but every person is different.

I am ten years old now, and I know there are many ways to help me live with hypermobility, as it will stay with me until I am a grown-up.

So, listen to your body and know that whatever is bothering you, it will get easier.

You've got this!

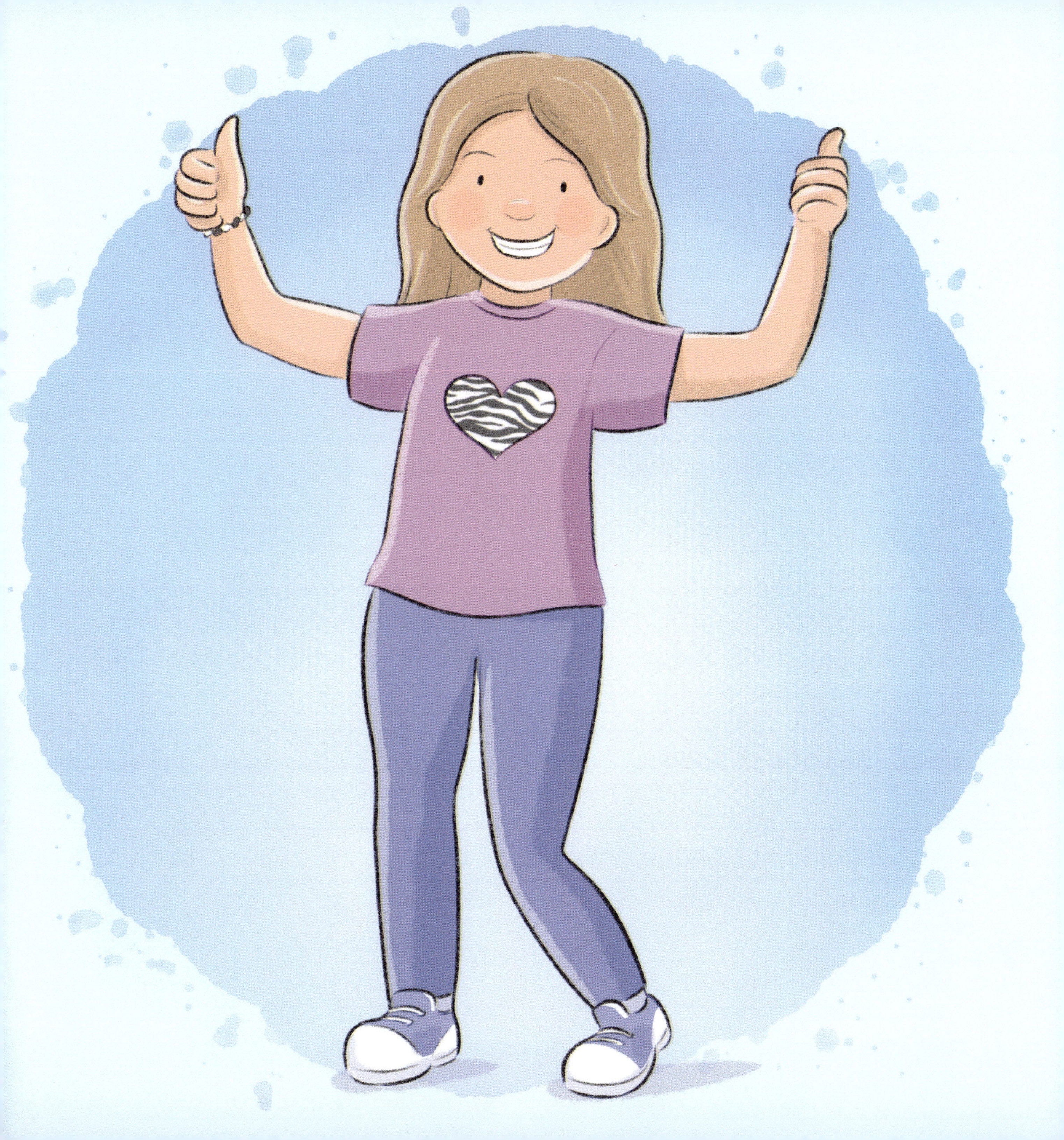

What is Joint Hypermobility Syndrome?

Joint Hypermobility Syndrome is a condition where one or more joints have an extra range of movement. It is also known as joint laxity or being double-jointed. It usually affects children and young people and often gets better as they get older. It is not an illness or a disease, just the way someone is put together.

It is usually normal and commonly seen in young children, with 5-15% of all UK school children being classed as hypermobile. In the majority of children, hypermobility will become less as they get older, but a small percentage will remain very flexible. This is more common if their parents are still very flexible. In most cases, hypermobility peaks at the age of five.

What are the symptoms of Joint Hypermobility Syndrome?

Children with Joint Hypermobility Syndrome may experience the following symptoms:

- Often get tired, even after rest
- Keep getting pain and stiffness in their joints or muscles
- Keep getting sprains and strains
- Keep dislocating their joints (they "pop out")
- Have poor balance or coordination
- Have thin, stretchy skin
- Have bladder or bowel problems

A GP will usually test for Joint Hypermobility Syndrome by checking the flexibility of the joints using a test called the Beighton scoring system. They may also refer the child for a blood test or X-ray to help rule out any other conditions, like arthritis.

How is Joint Hypermobility Syndrome treated?

There is no cure for Joint Hypermobility Syndrome. The main treatment is improving muscle strength and fitness, so the joints are better protected. A GP may refer the child to a physiotherapist, occupational therapist, or podiatrist for specialist advice. These physical therapies can help to reduce pain and the risk of dislocations, improve muscle strength and fitness, and improve posture and balance.

What can be done to help children with Joint Hypermobility Syndrome?

It is essential to increase the muscle strength around the affected joints, to provide additional support and improve joint stability. Low-impact exercise, such as swimming and cycling, will help maintain muscle strength, physical fitness, and well-being. Normal activities such as PE, playtime, and dance should be continued and encouraged. Children should not overextend their joints just because they can, and they should not do repetitive exercises or activities - take regular breaks (called pacing).

Here are some tips to help your child with Joint Hypermobility Syndrome at home:

1.) Exercise: Encourage your child to do low-impact exercises like swimming or cycling to improve joint and muscle strength and reduce strain. You can also try exercises that help improve proprioception (the ability to sense the position of a joint) and balance, such as Pilates. However, it is important to avoid overextending the joints and doing repetitive exercises or activities.

2.) Maintain a healthy weight: Being overweight can put extra strain on the joints, so it's important to maintain a healthy weight.

3.) Wear supportive shoes: Wearing supportive shoes can help stabilize hypermobile joints and improve posture and balance. If necessary, your podiatrist may recommend special insoles (orthotics) for your child's shoes.

4.) Take regular breaks: Encourage your child to take regular breaks during activities to avoid overextending the joints.

5.) Use heat therapy: Applying heat to the affected joints can help reduce pain and stiffness.

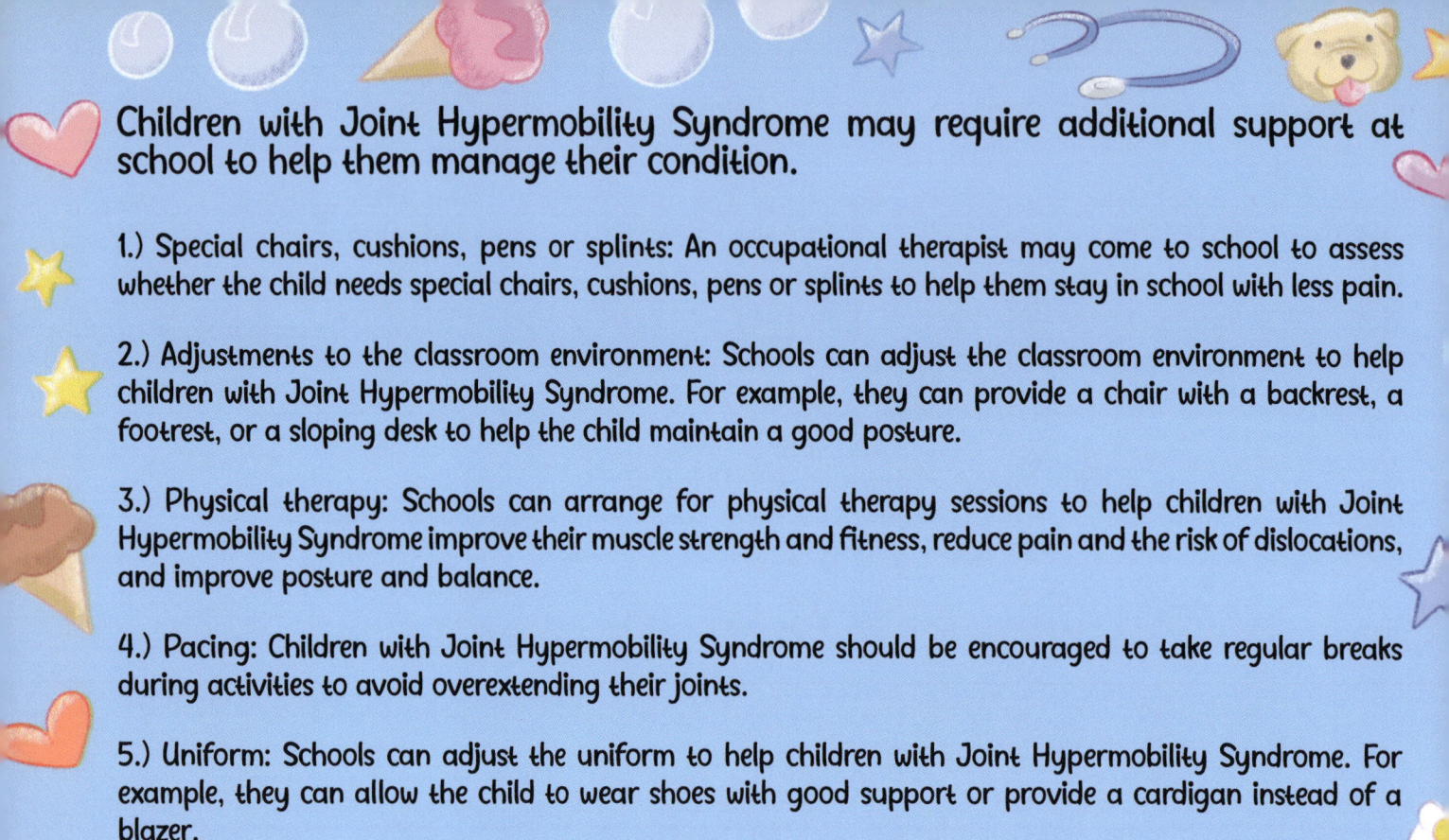

Children with Joint Hypermobility Syndrome may require additional support at school to help them manage their condition.

1.) Special chairs, cushions, pens or splints: An occupational therapist may come to school to assess whether the child needs special chairs, cushions, pens or splints to help them stay in school with less pain.

2.) Adjustments to the classroom environment: Schools can adjust the classroom environment to help children with Joint Hypermobility Syndrome. For example, they can provide a chair with a backrest, a footrest, or a sloping desk to help the child maintain a good posture.

3.) Physical therapy: Schools can arrange for physical therapy sessions to help children with Joint Hypermobility Syndrome improve their muscle strength and fitness, reduce pain and the risk of dislocations, and improve posture and balance.

4.) Pacing: Children with Joint Hypermobility Syndrome should be encouraged to take regular breaks during activities to avoid overextending their joints.

5.) Uniform: Schools can adjust the uniform to help children with Joint Hypermobility Syndrome. For example, they can allow the child to wear shoes with good support or provide a cardigan instead of a blazer.

6.) Toilet facilities: Schools can adjust the toilet facilities to help children with Joint Hypermobility Syndrome. For example, they can provide a raised toilet seat or a step to help the child reach the toilet.

How can I talk to my child's teacher about Joint Hypermobility Syndrome?

You can talk to your child's teacher about Joint Hypermobility Syndrome by explaining the condition and how it affects your child. You can also provide them with information about the condition, such as this book. Here are some tips to help you communicate effectively with your child's teacher:

1.) Schedule a meeting: Schedule a meeting with your child's teacher to discuss the condition and how it affects your child. This will give you an opportunity to explain the condition in detail and answer any questions the teacher may have.

2.) **Provide information:** Provide the teacher with information about Joint Hypermobility Syndrome. This will help the teacher understand the condition and how it affects your child.

3.) **Explain your child's needs:** Explain to the teacher how Joint Hypermobility Syndrome affects your child and what kind of support they may need in the classroom. For example, your child may need special chairs, cushions, pens, or splints to help them stay in school with less pain.

4.) **Collaborate with the teacher:** Work with the teacher to come up with a plan to help your child manage their condition at school. This may involve adjusting the classroom environment, arranging for physical therapy sessions, or providing additional support for your child.

What is the best way to explain Joint Hypermobility Syndrome to my child?

Explaining Joint Hypermobility Syndrome to a child can be challenging. Here are some tips that may help:

1.) **Keep it simple:** Use simple language and avoid medical jargon. Explain the condition in a way that your child can understand.

2.) **Use visual aids:** Use pictures or diagrams to help your child understand what Joint Hypermobility Syndrome is and how it affects their body.

3.) **Be honest:** Talk openly with your child about the condition and how it may affect them. Encourage them to ask questions and express their feelings.

4.) **Focus on the positive:** Emphasize that Joint Hypermobility Syndrome is not a disease and that it can be managed with proper care and treatment.

5.) **Encourage self-care:** Teach your child how to take care of themselves and their joints. Encourage them to exercise regularly, maintain a healthy weight, and wear supportive shoes.

It is important to listen to your child when they are explaining how they feel because it helps them feel valued and respected. When children feel that their parents or caregivers are listening to them, it builds their self-esteem, independence, confidence, and even their attention span. Listening to children also allows them to approach you more easily and build a relationship around trust.

About the Author

Leah Pinnington is thrilled to introduce her very first children's book.

With a heart full of imagination and a passion for storytelling, Leah has poured her creativity into crafting this true story.

As a child, Leah always had a deep love for books and still reads regularly. She particularly enjoys thriller, suspense, and mystery fiction.

During the writing process of this book, Leah discovered a newfound joy in bringing characters and the story to life. This journey of creating her first book has been filled with excitement, learning, and countless revisions.

Keep an eye out for more stories from Leah Pinnington in the future, as she continues to explore the limitless possibilities of children's literature.

Printed in Great Britain
by Amazon